Beda Higgins *Beda* x

Ourselves

Indigo Dreams Publishing

First Edition: Ourselves
First published in Great Britain in 2020 by:
Indigo Dreams Publishing
24, Forest Houses
Cookworthy Moor
Halwill
Beaworthy
Devon
EX21 5UU

www.indigodreams.co.uk

ISBN 978-1-912876-42-6

British Library Cataloguing in Publication Data. A CIP record for this book can be obtained from the British Library.

Designed and typeset in Palatino Linotype by Indigo Dreams.
Cover image by Tom Higgins.
Printed and bound in Great Britain by 4edge Ltd.

Papers used by Indigo Dreams are recyclable products made from wood grown in sustainable forests following the guidance of the Forest Stewardship Council.

For ourselves: in sickness and in health

Acknowledgements

The following poems have appeared previously:
The Heron, Winchester Poetry; *When She Qualified*, Onslaught Press; *Matilda The Skeleton*, Biscuit Publishing; *Wet 'n' Wild*, Biscuit Publishing; *The Demon Drink*, Mslexia Publications; *Lizzy (Loss)*, Zebra Publishing; *Til Death Do Us Part* (Strange Beasts), Bloodaxe Books; *Rebellion* and *Last Throw of the Dice*, Fair Acre Press.

A big thanks to my team of proof readers: Greg Kerr, Kath Mannix, Claire Bourke and Anna Lavigne; Will Mackie for nudges along the way; Rachel Bell for poetry events; Bernard, for being there; Ronnie and Dawn at IDP (and Geraldine), for the generous Geoff Stevens Award.

Grateful thanks to Tom Higgins for the cover design.

I owe a particular debt of gratitude to Joe Higgins for his patience and careful consideration in helping me put this collection together.

Also by Beda Higgins

Chameleon: Short Stories, Iron Press, 2011
Little Crackers: Short Stories, Saraband, 2014

CONTENTS

Ourselves

MY FIRST

I was taken behind drawn curtains
To witness a strange ceremony.
'African admission of no fixed address'
A blocked bed. He was stripped naked.

Watch and learn nurse:
Sponge with soap and water
Dry and plug the orifices, fix the teeth
Close and fasten the shroud.

I saw his dark skin iced white in freesia talc
His body rolled unknown in stiff grey paper
Knotted and tied as a cut of butcher's meat.
Here, he was not only dead: he was lost.

BE A GOOD VISITOR

It is wise to be ignorant, don't learn proper words
Be in awe of oedema and metastasis
Stick to growths, lumps and bumps.
Never look them in the eye and leave promptly
Seconds after the bell rings.

Ignore charts, smile briefly. Don't hold their gaze
Or dare *excuse me* at the office door.
Be blind to flecks of dirt and blood
Don't be emotional and wave I love you
Keep on the straight and narrow corridor.

Smile over cold scrambled eggs and dead flowers.
Don't ask could they have pain relief
Or be moved somewhere quiet.
Examine your thumbs and hum softly.
Bring boxes of chocolates, often.

WHAT EVA THINKS

Rain straight from the sky tastes sweet
Avocado's a fruit that should be a vegetable
Mermaids like to dry their hair in the wind
It's curly and blue so sailors can't see them
My big sister and her boyfriend sunbathe
With the tele on, no clothes, late at night
My Mum's in hospital and her head is shiny
A woodpecker knocks cuckoo can I come in
Seahorses don't know if they're a boy or a girl
Candyfloss is made when bees cough
My Mum's insides sound like crunchy crisps
A gazebo is half giraffe and a bit monkey
Grown-ups go woolly when they get old
Dew is sequins dropped after fairy parties
My heart has drum, I hear it playing
Some cats like to swim but can't
My Mum is sleepy and smells of pear-drops
Mexican beans jump because they're happy
Icicles taste dirty. Waterproof cagoules aren't
My Mum won't die because she loves me.

DOCTOR JONES

He was yellow, in his eyes and skin: a mizzler
   –   Medicine wasn't for him. His father a doctor, his before
Shoved him down a one-way alley, no U turns, no going back.

In drawers, plastic bags and high shelves he learnt
A new language, and held it close in prayers of comfort;
Parables and hymns: barbiturate, valium, pethidine and heroin.

Stick-thin and itchy he roamed days in the dead of night
Rising from a murky forest with shrugged apologies
His bruises told their own story.

We watched him darken like a kipper on the turn
The canteen lady begging the week before he died:
Lord above doctor, will you look after yerself?

ANOREXIC DAUGHTER

Take a mindo seed from our secret place
I've hidden it, exactly where it always was
Behind the pantry door. Be gentle it's delicate
Squeeze the leaves and smell the sea.
In a bite of salty breath, remember the care
Of your mother teaching you to cook
Instead of swim.
When you forget, smells can help
To remember our good moments.
Copy me again, these swollen joints;
Don't squash the mindo, you'll lose us
We've already been lost too long.
The bite should taste of the earth before sunset
Trickling evening shade warm and sleepy.
Lick your lips before dark closes on my kitchen,
When you feel ready, please eat.
Learn a new way to swim.

REBELLION

One wayward cell suggests a mutiny.
Before you know it, they are telling you
What will happen, and that it won't go away.

You shake and leave to live on the edge
Teetering in the mouth of a volcano.
On TV there is war. A building collapses.
It is very dark. Rescuers wear masks
So they aren't infected. You envy them.

You lie with your ear pressed to the ground
Head idling grass. You ignore planes soaring
Dogs yapping, an ambulance screaming blue panic
And listen to the earth groan gently on its axis.
There is comfort in the silence of earthworms.

A MOMENT

I take an old woman a glass of water
She has few pleasures left in life.
It's cold and sharp
Hill spring it says on the bottle.
She cups the tumbler as a chalice
And sips from a mountain spring
As a child she'd drunk in streams.
She smiles at the genie inside
And offers me a taste: it's sweet.
I hand it back and we make a toast
Fingers touching around the glass
Careful not to spill one drop of magic.

MARTYRS

The wheels spins in random selection:
One by one the doctor spreads a pack of cards
Whatever the cut, the Ace of Spades.
He shuffles results, dealing them out
Hands held close to his chest, and opens play.
I watch his eyes and think he's bluffing.
St Agnes cut her breasts off and served them
On a plate, nipple up, I get that – and gamble
With God: let me live and they're all yours.

After, I have one male and one female.
My boy is hard and lacks tenderness
Flat-mannered and straight-forward
He doesn't flout, pout or point, and with only
The slightest swell, he hardly ruffles blouses
Falling in closed curtains, his show is over.
His tight-lipped scar sniggers at my girl
Who is soft and doe-like, drooping dozily
She is clumsy and gets in the way
A slave to moods, she sulks and nags
'til I'm sore with her pulling and silk and lace
Neediness: *we are still a woman, aren't we?*

IN THE EYE OF THE STORM

Home from his shift, the latch clicks, she hears and switches
Supper to warm for fifteen minutes chat, a glass of wine
And pauses to say: How was your day?

He goes to change, bewildered by pouring sweat
Memories of those faces, blood trickling out between his hands
Sympathy in eyes: *You were first on the scene?*

Shock flashbacks smack when he's least expecting
Late at night, early morning, bolt upright on replay
What if's? Maybe? If I'd given?

He listens to work banter, nights out and gigs,
Goes home – now alone. Head in hands, he's no cook
And simmers for hours reducing himself

    –   Down to the bone and grizzle of their rusting blood.

FOOTSTEPS

There are corridors we walk in solidarity
Shoulder to shoulder, hip to hip, heads high
Lace-up shoes squeaking on buffed green floors.

My mother and sisters' lanterns go before me.
Our woollen cloaks swirl through the dead of night.
I follow their ghost steps tapping at my heart:

If all that's left when you're shaking with shock or
Sorrow or frustration or bone marrow tiredness:
Lift your chin, with your best foot forward.

MAYBE TODAY

I'd like to walk down the street and no one notice me
To brush shoulders, bump arms – no head turns
Or sad puppy eyes following my stooped back
    –   Only my shadow keeping a close eye on me.
Ordinary days of opening curtains, radio music
A bit of shopping with coffee and cake stops.
I'll skim the surface of life, a bit ungainly but
No one will care; they'll assume I'm bald by choice.
I won't be tired, and my lips won't crack
No headaches or floppy heads mewling:
How are you my Dear?

AND

The baby cries hungry for other than food
And she rubs eyes but not for lack of sleep
And the toddler pees but not for a potty
And tablets are gulped but not for pain
And doctor visits but the bell doesn't work
And health workers scribble without saying a word
And doors slam not for needing to be shut
And he swigs vodka but isn't thirsty
And social carers write, but there are no reports
And neighbours draw curtains, but it isn't night
And case-conferences are called but not convened
And friends haven't seen them but they're not blind
And needles are readied but not to sew and mend
And now, too weak to cry, another baby dies.

I HAVE A QUESTION

Can I put my geraniums out?
Or do I have to wade through appointments and
Phone messages: My call is important to them.

Can I steal my hidden cache of dormant roots
Dip fingers in dry peat, sweep cobwebs
And wonder at their twitch of life,

Or do I have to give blood, go to hospital
Wait in stuffy rooms crowded with worry
And look as if I understand what they tell me.

Can I breathe the dusky scent of childhood
My mother pruning with a silly hat on
While I hop, trying to learn how to skip.

I pack a small case and lie on a thin bed
Beginning a twelve-month life-sentence
Imprisoned in treatment and side-effects.

My dreams hibernate in a cool dark place.
I live to tip pots, stroke open veins and
Dig holes in wet soil with bare hands.

SAME OLD

When I was little I was given a black dolly.
She had a blue maid's outfit, white shiny eyes
And the packet said: with golly hair.

Cindy and Barbie sneered hard plastic, and no
Matter how I arranged and sorted the toy box
    –   Golden and thin, they wouldn't let her be.

My first ward; all the cleaners were black.
And in every face
The truth I'd seen in her eyes, was blinking back.

HAGGLING

The hospital rings: there's been an incident.
They run – falling into a white bright room
Where nurses flick pin-ball machines
Pinging round and round.

Lying tangled with outstretched arms
Their crucified son is carried down-river
He rolls back, stranded on grey matter:
They see headstones in his eye sockets.

Hope snaps when the medics open market
    –   A doctor with Mr Happy socks comes in to trade:
Heavy sacks of sympathy for his kidneys
Nods of respect for his heart and lungs

Pouring tea with gentle hums of persuasion

    –   For the silent and invisible who wait.

'TIL DEATH DO US PART

In the dayroom crooked mouths open and close,
Discussing sore knees with small sequinned eyes.
Photograph stills in sepia grey, their translucent skins
And blue lips drift off into shallow sleeps,
Woken by the gong to paddle in for lunch.

It's quorn sausage and mash today.
Archie, what manner of meat is quorn?
Unicorn I think Margaret.
She smiles stroking his liver-spotted hand,
And ties a ribboned soft sigh in a bow of love.

HER NAME IS MERCY

Fifteen years old and she wants to be someone.
It's silent inside, she has nothing to say.
He drinks in her mouth and gropes her dress
For a heart that drowned when they married.

A tight placental membrane binds her;
 Family honour ties her arms
And tethers her legs.
She takes short dainty steps – no cracks on show.

Hearing freedom whispered she runs –
Skin on sweaty skin, the can shut tight.
Breathing others' breath, she prays 'til they prize
The tin open and peel her out like a clam.

Down a dark stairwell on a line of mattresses
Marinated in vodka and dished up on stained sheets
They sniff to check she's still fresh.
At sixteen, she knows she is no one.

LEAVING

He ignores unbuttoned blouses, lost lists
She always had a dreamy way of thinking.
He notices her hop, slip and jump
Lifting a spoon to cut her toast.

In their bed she follows a map of stars
And shifts drifting whispers,
He holds on tight to anchor her
And tries to stop her floating away.

With a short smile and worry-bitten knuckle
He takes her on the hottest day in August.
His journey home stretches on and on
Roads quiver and buckle in the heat.

RESPECT

You'd been my rock, I wanted to thank you
And was shocked to find you in that wrecked hole:
Blistering walls covered in rashes, infected with rot

The pipes belched foul air,
No-one answered the phones, computers said *NO*
And constipated staff were full of shite.

How are you Prof?

Before you could speak
A square-faced nurse bustled in brandishing business
Hands on hips: "Not again you mucky Pup".

It felt like a bad film – I knew what was going on
But it couldn't be happening?

You bowed, broken; shreds of dignity lay in tatters
I blanched and spat: Get Out!
Doesn't she know? You are a fine man.

CANDLE

Test after test the woman feels her warm body grow cold
    –   the fuse blown.
Each month endlessly beginning and ending again
In a grinning smear of failure on her pants.

She sets out on her pilgrimage
Nursing a belly of fear; it's her last chance.
On the train a baby sucks a fat bosom
Her chest aches to be full of milk.

She swallows her folic acid – a dot of hope
And shuffles with lame and maimed to beg.
Kneeling at the feet of St Gerard
She lights a candle and prays.

She waits
And waits.

DON'T THINK – JUST DO

Evolutionary blips or too young to decide?
Eyes caught by surprise: who am I?
Bisexual transgender neutral pan or gay?

They come in camouflage, T shirts and jeans
For prescribed hormones to up-surge their delicate balance
I push the syringe wincing: *is this the best we can do?*

My head drifts to foggy tales of past practice
    –   Nurses asked to pass metal instruments
For gods in surgical games of Russian roulette:

Shiny knives and cleaves to crack open skulls
Lopping off psychosis, cutting and carving
To cast out egos, leaving half-brained half-wits

No-one would bother to report as missing.
Did those nurses falter as splatter brains hit the bucket
    –   And dare to question: *is this the best we can do?*

A STROKE OF BAD LUCK

He soaks up stares, mouth drooping
Dreading those words:
How are you Michael? His name is Mark.

He goes back to the beginning, ABC
Letters splash, puddling meaning; maybe foreign?
He threads words onto strings, but they slip off
    –   Tries the phone but the wires are cut
So he listens carefully to the radio for hints.

Nursery rhymes and prayers see-saw
Our Father Who Art in Heaven back and forth:
Chants and rote, barely keeping him afloat.

THE WORLD STOPS

She sees nothing, hears everything
Heavy and waiting as if she's swallowed a rock
    –   And is still expected to float.
They wash, dry, and swaddle him
Hand him over with downcast eyes
As a parcel – to soften the truth.
She circles his face, fingers imprinting to memory
Soft curves and swells carved into her heart.
With utmost care she peels the blankets one by one
Until she can bend and breathe his skin
A kiss
    –   smashes her shell
Spineless and speechless, surrounded in
Broken fragments sharp as glass.
She picks at pieces
Bits of the night, hours of voices
A mirage of rippling dead faces
    –   The morning caught in her son's hair
A curling lock, she wraps in blue ribbon.

A WISH AND A PRAYER

Two puckered kids race over pigeon droppings
Their chattering feet shriek into thin air.
Milo squeaks on a rusty pogo stick
Jake sits on mildew, acned with wet moss, and
Wishes he had a coat, maybe even a Parka;
He picks his scabs, waiting for a turn.
Milo jumps high and says he'll live forever,
He's their Mam's favourite and has an anorak.
Jake keeps his ears deaf under a balaclava
It's pink, but inside his head feels warm.
Drizzly sun splits a dazzling rainbow
Jake stands on tip-toes and makes a wish.

INFORMED CHOICE

Maybe she will, maybe she won't
But if she drinks enough
    –   She doesn't have to decide.
She swanks into the club on heady platform shoes
Her mouth chews butter, forever melting
And downs bottle after bottle
Breaking glass, throwing up
Falling down
Tit over arse.
Waking spongy from the night before she hears
Someone cough, cracking songs into the frying pan.
She sit opposite him at the table; maybe it's John?
Stirs orange juice with paracetamol and nurofen
The smell of wildcat sprayed between them
She aches from sex
She can't remember, and sucks peaches from a tin
Scooping out a slippery Friday night.
Her forehead tight, stretched with effort; it could be Jim?

AWOL

You clap hands with lightbulb eyes
And spark electricity from flipper palms
Showing me how it shoots.

Electrodes and amps are useful you say
But you generate from your own body
I watch your arms whirl as you shine.

Illuminated, you tell of satellites orbiting and
Voices tuning in. Glowing bright, short-circuiting
You fuse a brain that hasn't slept in weeks.

LIZZY

God took a measuring tape and laid your life flat
Cutting out a patchwork pattern.
Minutes and hours nipped off
Bunching days into smaller moments.

You keep cuttings and threads as keepsakes
Travelling in books, across lands in chapters
Running barefoot over your bed
Miles journeyed popped under pillows.

God tucks and pleats. You concertina into
Confined spaces, a gauged length
Your room is twelve steps across
And fourteen shuffles wide.

You watch your life from the window
    –   They turn and wave. You slip smiles
In your handkerchief, it's never goodbye.
You measure loss, but the tape isn't long enough.

THEN AND NOW

He shook his serviette and spread it over his knees
Considering the menu, before giving his order
To the handsome waiter:
A full cooked breakfast, eggs over easy.

Hart shut his eyes for three seconds long
To snap his daydream in two;
There was no hope for a man who noticed
Cheekbones and chocolate eyes.

He checked his watch, soon all would be well
He would drown without wailing
Or rippling the metal grey water
Stretching on and on beyond blue.

The waiter placed his plate with shy smile
In a different world Hart might fall in love
But for this battle his self-loathing had won
     –   He was done.

He poured his tea with a tremor
Which could easily be the ebb of the sea
And topped up with vodka
His holy water kept in an inside pocket.

He ate slowly
Wishing it was the boy's red lips he chewed
And carefully mopped up the last of his eggs
Before patting his chin with a flag of surrender.

Hart stepped up on deck for a stroll
And thanked the young waiter
Who never forgot the man with fog in his eyes
  –   Stepping over-board.

A friend rang and told me: it's on Facebook
He killed himself
With his whole life in front of him.
Him Crane me Cusack, we sat next to each other at school.

Year nine, his desk empty for weeks – mumbling glandular fever
He blushed when I teased him for schmoozing
Knowing it wasn't girls. Sometimes we had a laugh
One Christmas a kiss.

HOW

Flopped across the bed, staring into space
"For TLC only" red marks your notes.
You look so normal
Despite the abnormal blood tests, the shadowy X-ray
The cup of tea left cold, maybe no-one noticed.

You go absent without leave, an egg-timer ticking away hours
Falling through a small gap and unable to get out.
Dissolving minutes you don't move apart from grains;
Twitches of air
Ear lobes flinching, piss trickling, it's too hard to shit.

Wordless, soundless, endless – a dead weight.
In an eclipse, before the world darkens, birds are struck dumb
Knowing it will happen.
How can I make my lips move to speak:
I know what is coming.

MATILDA THE SKELETON

Matilda doesn't bat an eyelid as strip-teasing fingers
Stroke her long legs, white and smooth.

In the sweaty walled chamber, flaking skin dust
They breathe in and out, open-mouthed, green ghosted.

A thumb prises her jaw open, rubbing her teeth
Her vertebrae a xylophone, plinked and plonked.

Strangers handling her pelvis, counting her toes
Feeling her fingers, learning her insides out.

Middle of her ribcage a serrated breast-bone
Vexes; but her wide shocked sockets say it all:

He'll say in court: *she hadn't me tea ready.*

THE DEMON DRINK

With wide lapels and turn-up trousers, he licks the creamy
head off his black and white pint and lights a fag fat-fingered.
She makes a pastry pie and lassoes chuckles off the radio
popping socks to dry on the stove, she wipes the table clean.
Across tambourine mountains he sings loud an open mouth
of sunshine, echoing relics of kids and cows in the field.
She polishes kitchen steps waiting for the tea to brew and
uses a china tea-pot, jug, cup and saucer; it was her mother's.
He smiles punch drunk at the barmaid, his wife has eggshell
nerves, tapping the side of his head, he implies she could crack
any minute. She slices tongue and ham sandwiches with crinkle
cut beetroot, the daisies in the bottle look nice against the pink
and purple meat. He gallops a story up Irish summer hills
dizzy with blarney, cantering years, leaping fences of craic
dealing cards and lies. She hums bringing the washing in,
tall trees yawn in an orange sky. He tries to light a spent
match, and rubs his purple ear thinking he hears a banjo, his
feet follow an old jig to the twanging tune. The barmaid
frowns, hennaed hair bristling: *time, gentlemen please.*
Fading hours burn in the grate of drunk men's past; he laughs.
She waters and nips, sowing seeds of Sweetheart Peas.
He has a piss and pulls his stretchy pants up, no zips or belt,
what a grand idea they are, and ignoring the ditch of greasy
mud he slips. She watches a dusky star hold a pulse of life
twinkling through the bedroom window, their unmade sheets
tangling love and hate. Slumped in a stinking side street
downed and pale, he kisses curled leaves with his arse under
dark-bellied clouds: *This is her fucking fault. Her fault for giving
me fucking rabbit food instead of meat so there's nowt to sop up the
beer. I'll fucking teach her, my fucking keks got wet and stink from the*

muck, from the fucking ditch, bitch. He rams his message hard 'til
she knows and won't forget, on her knees, he's seriously
hacked off. A diamond day cuts through curtains, lighting a
trickle down her cheek. She takes the ring off, it's too heavy
and packs her case in sighs. He pulls his dirty collar
the tide-mark rubbing his stubble, and gags on last night's
guilty sex, he'll give up for good today he'll get her back
and stirs his second Bloody Mary with bitter salty tears.

WHEN SHE QUALIFIED

She learnt to juggle hours
To listen to ghosts, hear confessions
To pick out nits and sew with dreams.

To patch a memory knit with notions
To be a mouse creeping in cracks
To forage and eat shades of grey.

To be wide-eyed day and night
To beetle hard-shelled, to learn
To love the comfort of cold walls.

To be another face in a sea of faces
To forget what day her birthday is
To be godless but yearn to pray.

LAST RIGHTS

I don't float or throb in soft lights
No high note of swooping bat calls.
There's no purgatory queue
Waiting for a pearly thumbs-up, or
Reincarnation in soulful cats' eyes.
Don't burden me with unrequited love
Or God forbid, confession at my bed
With vigils of flickering candles.
I hear your laments and I'm moved
    –   But tired. I keep my eyes closed
And like Vaseline rubbed on my lips.
While I'm dying, please let me live.

HAPPY HAPPY HAPPY

Yellow yawns on a lion's mane shaking out the morning mist it
muzzles earth aside
Piercing winter with darts of daffs that open grinning along
park benches and
Garden gates dancing cha cha cha and stops for lemonade
sharp and sweet fizzing
Stripy bees dripping honey and buzzing to the flashing Pelican
crossing for sallow-
Skinned pensioners on strolls to feed Easter chicks over cool gin
and tonic with
A ring of lemon coward soldiers dipped in runny yolks spilling
onto a horizon of
Desert sands shifting Eastern promise where a golden god
smiles on acres of corn
Floating in bowls of crunchy happy mornings vitamins for the
day and pills that
Stop Mummy being sad so she can smile and stroke her straw-
haired child battery-
Fed nuggets chips vanilla ice-cream screen-time and no dreams
he shoots the breeze
And soaring high he spins and springs their fourth-floor
window: *I can fly.*

HYPOCRITES

We nurse his greedy cancer as if our hearts will break
When it finally gives up eating him alive.
We pander to its whims, dress and mop, pack
Oozing wounds, offer it pain relief, relaxant,
Balm and salve for ragged nerves.

This quiet gentle man becomes a stranger.
He rattles bedside cots, grasps and dribbles
Flashes his withered balls and gasps air, his mouth
Becomes a gaping fish hole. He mumbles: *fuck*
His wife has never heard him swear and weeps.

And at each shift, we wish he was dead.

WHAT MONEY CAN'T BUY

At the private school where conversations
Are dished up on dainty plates
She's handed her passport to meet nice people
And visas for parties in hotel parlours
Recipes for soufflés and table setting
How to correctly swan-fold serviettes.

Her Father visits and watches, enchanted.
Dignity, manners, and time-honoured virtue.
She crosses her legs, smooths her long skirt
Attentively listens with solemn large eyes.
She rarely sleeps and cuts her arms for relief.
He's pleased with what money can buy.

IN FOR TESTS

She lies on a sick bed-roll, her locker
Full of frightened tissues and sweaty sweets.
Bowls of bananas freckle into blotched melanomas
And daffodils shriek: we're all ill in here y 'know!

She flicks by hours in magazine make-overs
And listens to whispers behind shallow screens
Of scars and plastic bags, a baby born with
No head, and bog-eyed nights out.

Tea's wheeled in and she frets for her purse
It's alright Pet, this one is on the house.
At lunch she has jelly – the first time in years
Each spoonful quivers as if it's her last.

WET 'N' WILD

Stamped with love-bites and swollen lips a boy plays with his girlfriend's ringed belly-button, she pushes forward damp in her gold bikini. Prawns of boys shoulder each others' acne, a man wears tight trunks permed hair and leather skin, his medallion rusts. It rains and rains, wet with sweat, a limp plastic palm tree wilts weary with it all. Nans and Mams waggle on the same dimpled legs, cloned freckled backs, broad hips, body fuzz fizzes, tattoos prickle and spread over arms and thighs, shoulders are legs of birds, eagles, fish and anchors. Aging skin puckers with a splattering of peppercorn blackheads ripe for squeezing. An octopus of arms and legs flail over silver swimming shoals. Dee sits sticky in the café with bags of food, she eats red in the face watching clouds slap the water through shards of glass. Pony-tailed girls fold arms across flat chests and lads stare down bigger arses, running with the smells of underarms and sour sex soaking. Sharon with her sprayed scrunchie leans into Wayne; cool gods like Becks and Posh heavy with petting. Breasted men with pregnant bellies waddle too big for their feet. Two skinny kids go to the café, poke tin-foil parcels, she waits for them to leave and eats theirs too. A cross-eyed man swivels a pogo-stick lurch, he's given a wide berth in case it's catchy. A pikey with yellow and black hair buzzes and head-butts. Blue knobbly-knees and hairpin elbows hold a cold matchstick girl together, her eyes skim the water; shivering. Dee troughs and swallows the final doughnut without chewing; wishes she wasn't and that he hadn't. Spit floats, fluffing the water. Daniel in armbands is scared. He learnt about germs when he had chemo. Everyone turns, everyone stares: he's still bald. He takes a deep breath and turns to wave: Someone should feel happy.

THE FUSE LIT

His land lay splattered in war wounds
Slit trenches, amputated tree stumps
Swollen veins and bleeding rivers.

His city disembowelled, tents erected
As a row of colostomy bags; dead
Bodies are the waste products of war.

Gum chewing a metallic taste of bullets
He's set on a timer, heart shooting
Rat-a-tat-tat, he could go off any minute.

IN THE COUNTRY

She smuggles the wet creature deep in her coat
Out from the barn of stained hay

Into a cold shrinking evening
    –   Drops it in a ditch

And watches it kick
A kind of jellyfish with head and legs.

Hedges bow with mantilla cobwebs
Peering down at the new-born shining pale.

It hurt more than when she broke her wrist
She hopes she won't burn in hell.

LAST THROW OF THE DICE

Drug pierce your burning skin
Everyone is the enemy:
Why me? When? How long?

Flotsam cells trail sweats and bad tastes
Mind blurring, befuddled
You wonder how horses sleep standing up.

Learning to accept, you watch the sunrise
And flick newspapers
With a fresh interest in obituaries.

Melt chocolate in your fissured mouth and
Watch *Strictly Come Dancing* to have
Something to believe in and talk about.

You touch bluebells pulled from dark woods,
The petals hold the moon's long, soft kiss:
A small white skull of being here.

TREATS

The shop lady knocks, she is posh with pearly lipstick
Her Botox arrow eyebrows shoot alarmingly high
Mavis likes to see that life is full of surprises.
She has thirty pence left for a last supper
And lifts her pin-cushioned puffed hand
Bruised and battered from the battle
To point at the Flake: *it's been years.*
She sits and shakily unwraps her treasure
Finger over bumps and smells the small log
Carefully collecting splinters that drop.
Her bloated pumpkin face shines
Grateful for the small gifts she has left.

HERON

For Maura, Steve, Gemma and Matt, in loving memory of Chris.

When you left he came
On water and air, at a distance
Still and silent, alone
Telling me bit by bit how it would be –
The hurt like water rippling – different every day
But the same shapes and colour
In the blue flow of me to you.
He raises his head high, lifting to fly
Wings wide open. I watch his reflection:
Him there, me here, and you always, skin close.
Some days I can almost touch you.

Indigo Dreams Publishing Ltd
24, Forest Houses
Cookworthy Moor
Halwill
Beaworthy
Devon
EX21 5UU
www.indigodreams.co.uk